Financial Institutions Outreach Initiative

Report on Outreach to Money Services Businesses
July 2010

Financial Institutions Outreach Initiative

Report on Outreach to Money Services Businesses

July 2010

Table of Contents

Executive Summary

The Financial Crimes Enforcement Network (FinCEN) is engaged in a variety of initiatives to ensure that our mission as administrator of the Bank Secrecy Act (BSA) is carried out in the most efficient and effective manner possible. In furtherance of these goals, FinCEN initiated an outreach effort in 2009 to money services businesses (MSBs), as part of a broader, ongoing effort to meet with representatives from a variety of industries that fall under BSA regulatory requirements. This outreach also assists in FinCEN's ongoing work with the financial industry as financial institutions strive to comply with their responsibility to focus their efforts, consistent with risks, to report certain financial information and suspicious activities to FinCEN, as well as our responsibility to ensure this useful information is made available to law enforcement, as appropriate.

The purpose of this report is to share insights FinCEN gathered during its outreach to large MSBs. Information contained in this report about practices and procedures that was obtained by FinCEN during the course of the outreach initiative does not imply FinCEN's approval of those practices, nor does it mean that FinCEN requires any financial institution to follow these examples. These findings have no effect on FinCEN's regulations or guidance. They may, however, be useful to MSBs interested to learn how other institutions are working to comply with similar regulatory responsibilities.

Among the key findings, FinCEN found that MSBs place significant emphasis on agent oversight and compliance. An overarching theme discussed by the MSBs was that maintaining their reputation and the trust of their customers is the core objective of their business models, and that being in compliance with BSA regulations is consistent with their business model.

Many of the MSBs noted that while there is a heavy emphasis on establishing BSA compliance policies and designing training curricula, their primary concentration of resources is implementation of procedures, including at the agent level. In that regard, it may be of interest to note the use of "mystery shopping visits" by some MSBs to test their agents' compliance with BSA requirements. In addition, MSBs raised issues regarding regulatory examinations. While the Bank Secrecy Act/Anti-Money Laundering Examination Manual was released only shortly before FinCEN's outreach began, MSBs expressed an interest in continuing to improve the coordination and centralization of examinations.

The MSBs also identified additional guidance that they would like to see from FinCEN that would be helpful in fulfilling their anti-money laundering (AML) program requirements, particularly regarding prepaid access.

Both FinCEN and the MSBs found the outreach meetings to be very valuable. This report also contains an overview of BSA/AML requirements for MSBs, along with information about other available resources.

Introduction

In 2008, FinCEN launched an outreach initiative to learn more about the business practices of financial institutions, how their AML programs operate, and the challenges of implementing these programs, in order to enhance our ability to ensure the consistent application of, examination for, and enforcement of the BSA.

This initiative was intended to obtain information that would contribute to a broader understanding of financial industry practices, and what financial institutions need in order to effectively implement their AML programs. FinCEN's outreach began with meetings during 2008 with some of the nation's largest financial institutions. The report on FinCEN's findings from this initiative was published in October 2009.[1]

After this phase of our outreach, we determined that the next industry group FinCEN would meet with would be MSBs. Specifically, in the 2009 outreach initiative to MSBs, FinCEN representatives sought to better understand how the MSB's AML programs operated, both technically and analytically, as well as how AML compliance was integrated into the MSB's business plan.

MSBs play a critical role in providing financial services to, among others, a segment of the population that generally may not have access to bank accounts. Law enforcement, FinCEN, and other Federal regulators repeatedly stress the need to prevent transactions that typically flow through these businesses from going underground, which would diminish transparency with respect to these transactions. Because MSBs provide needed financial services to numerous communities throughout the country and often facilitate the transmission of money to those in foreign countries, they are vital to both domestic and foreign economies.

FinCEN obtained listings of the nation's largest MSBs from two of our state banking regulatory partners, and conducted an analysis of the MSBs with the greatest number of BSA filings. From these lists, FinCEN identified 13 MSBs that collectively represented a cross-section of MSB activities.

---

1. See http://www.fincen.gov/news_room/rp/reports/pdf/Bank_Report.pdf

Once the MSBs were identified, we sent a letter to the appropriate senior official within each MSB to outline the goals of the FinCEN outreach initiative and invite the MSB's voluntary participation.

Between March and September 2009, interdisciplinary teams from FinCEN visited nine MSBs in conjunction with this outreach effort. The remaining MSBs were not visited, either because of scheduling difficulties or other extenuating circumstances.

Although FinCEN reached out generally to these financial institutions to participate in the outreach initiative, each MSB was asked to develop its own agenda for the meeting. Accordingly, the topics covered and issues discussed with each MSB varied.

This report summarizes the information gathered by FinCEN during the course of the outreach to the nation's largest MSBs. In order to safeguard the proprietary business information provided by the MSBs, no company names are used within this report.

FinCEN would like to express its appreciation to all the MSBs and the staff that devoted their time and effort to participate in this outreach initiative. FinCEN team members found all of the meetings to be very informative and valuable to furthering FinCEN's broader mission of enhancing U.S. national security, deterring and detecting criminal activity, and safeguarding financial systems from abuse by promoting transparency in the U.S. and international financial systems.

Background on BSA and AML Programs

The BSA[2] was enacted by the U.S. Congress in 1970 in response to concern over the use of financial institutions by criminals to launder the proceeds of their illicit activity. The BSA has been amended on several occasions, most significantly by the Money Laundering Control Act (MLCA) of 1986[3] and Title III of the USA PATRIOT Act of 2001.[4]

The BSA authorizes the Secretary of the Treasury, *inter alia*, to issue regulations requiring financial institutions to keep certain records and file certain reports,[5] and to implement anti-money laundering programs and compliance procedures to guard against money laundering.[6] The authority of the Secretary to administer the BSA has been delegated to the Director of FinCEN.[7] The BSA's overarching goal is to "require certain reports or records where they have a high degree of usefulness in criminal, tax, or regulatory investigations or proceedings, or in the conduct of intelligence or counterintelligence activities, including analysis, to protect against international terrorism."[8]

While some requirements in the BSA and its implementing regulations apply to individual persons, most of the BSA's statutory and regulatory requirements apply to financial institutions.[9] The statute defines the term "financial institution" broadly.[10] It includes traditional financial institutions such as banks, securities broker-dealers, and insurance companies.[11] It also includes cash-intensive entities that handle significant amounts of currency such as casinos and MSBs, as well as entities not traditionally considered financial institutions but which engage in transactions that can also be vulnerable to money laundering, such as dealers in precious metals, stones, or jewels, and vehicle sellers.[12]

---

2. See http://www.fincen.gov/statutes_regs/bsa/ and Titles I and II of Public Law 91-508, as amended, codified at 12 U.S.C. §§1829b, 12 U.S.C. §§ 1951-1959, and 31 U.S.C. §§ 5311-5314, 5316-5332.

3. See Public Law 99-57 and 18 U.S.C §§ 1956 and 1957.

4. See Title III of Public Law 107-56, available at http://www.fincen.gov/statutes_regs/patriot/

5. See 31 U.S.C. §§ 5313 and 5318(g).

6. See 31 U.S.C. § 5318(h).

7. See Treasury Order 180-01 (Sept. 26, 2002).

8. See 31 U.S.C. § 5311.

9. See 31 U.S.C. § 5312(a)(2); 31 C.F.R. § 103.11(n).

10. See 31 U.S.C. § 5312 (a)(2).

11. See id.

12. See id.

The term MSB, as currently defined in the BSA regulations, refers to each of the following distinct categories of financial service providers: (1) Currency dealer or exchanger; (2) check casher, (3) issuer of traveler's checks, money orders, or stored value; (4) seller or redeemer of traveler's checks, money orders, or stored value; (5) money transmitter; and (6) the United States Postal Service.[13]

Like other financial institutions under the BSA, MSBs must implement AML programs. These programs, at a minimum, must include: the development of internal policies, procedures, and controls; designation of a compliance officer; an ongoing employee training program; and an independent review function to test programs.[14] BSA regulations also require certain MSBs to register with FinCEN and prepare and maintain a list of agents, if any.[15]

A MSB must file a Currency Transaction Report (CTR) (FinCEN Form 104)[16] for each transaction in currency[17] (deposit, withdrawal, exchange, or other payment or transfer) of more than $10,000 by, through, or to the MSB. A CTR must be filed for all single currency transactions of more than $10,000 by or on behalf of any one person in one business day.[18] Multiple currency transactions must be aggregated, and a CTR is required if the business has knowledge that the multiple transactions are by or on behalf of any person and result in currency in or out totaling more than $10,000 in one business day.[19]

A Suspicious Activity Report by Money Services Business (SAR-MSB) (FinCEN Form 109)[20] must be filed if a transaction is conducted or attempted by, at, or through an MSB, *and* it involves or aggregates funds or other assets of a least $2,000, *and* the MSB knows, suspects, or has reason to suspect that the transaction (or pattern of transactions):

- Involves funds derived from illegal activity, or is intended to hide or disguise funds or assets derived from illegal activity, as part of a plan to violate or evade any Federal law or regulations, or to avoid any transaction reporting requirement under Federal law or regulation;

---

13. See 31 CFR § 103.11(uu)(1) – (6).

14. See 31 U.S.C. § 5318(h).

15. See31 C.F.R. § 103.41.

16. See http://www.fincen.gov/forms/files/fin104_ctr.pdf.

17. Currency is defined as coin and paper money of the United States or of any other country that (1) is designated as legal tender, (2) circulates, and (3) is customarily used and accepted as a medium of exchange in the country of issuance. See 31 CFR § 103.11(h).

18. See 31 C.F.R. § 103.22(b)(1).

19. See 31 C.F.R. § 103.22 (c)(2)

20. See http://www.fincen.gov/forms/files/fin109_sarmsb.pdf

- Is designed, whether by structuring or other means, to evade any requirements of the BSA;

- Serves no business or apparent lawful purpose, and the reporting MSB knows of no reasonable explanation for the transaction after examining the available facts, including the background and possible purpose of the transaction; or Involves the use of the MSB to facilitate criminal activity.[21]

As administrator of the BSA, FinCEN has delegated authority to the IRS, another bureau of the Department of the Treasury, to examine the MSBs for compliance with BSA requirements.[22] Furthermore, Treasury Directive 15-41 delegates to the Commissioner of the IRS the authority to conduct BSA examinations of certain non-bank financial institutions, including MSBs, to assure compliance.[23]

Although the BSA is not directly enforced by State agencies, the examination process in some states evaluates compliance with Federal regulations, including the BSA. Additionally, State agencies are charged with enforcing state statutes and regulations that apply to MSBs, which may impose requirements that overlap with the BSA. Therefore, State regulators may examine MSBs for compliance with certain BSA requirements, possibly including compliance with the AML program requirement, as elements of a more comprehensive list of compliance requirements imposed under State law. These requirements, however, vary from state to state.

---

21. See 31 C.F.R. § 103.20.
22. See 31 C.F.R. § 103.56(b)(8).
23. See http://www.treasury.gov/regs/td15-41.htm

Business Volume/Scope

In meeting with many of the largest MSBs in the country, FinCEN gained insight into the products and services offered by these MSBs and the scope of their business operations. The following descriptions underscore that there is strong global demand for the financial services provided by the MSBs.

- One MSB noted it has offices in dozens of countries and operations in over 100 countries with hundreds of branches worldwide. In 2007, this MSB conducted nearly 20 million transactions.

- Another MSB focuses its product on payroll cards, which are used as a payroll distribution channel for its clients.

- One MSB indicated it has over 70 million active customer accounts, supports payments in over a dozen currencies, and has money transmitter licenses in most states.

- Another MSB that focuses on international money transfers noted it has thousands of agent locations globally in more than 100 countries and 5 continents, and is licensed in almost all U.S. states. In 2008, this MSB conducted millions of dollars of money transfer transactions in the United States, and even more money transfers globally.

- Another MSB offers a variety of services through a network of nearly 400,000 agent locations in 200 countries and territories.

- One MSB indicated that it sells approximately 186 million money orders each year.

- Another leading global payments services company noted it now had nearly 200,000 locations in approximately 200 countries and territories with revenues of over $1.0 billion in 2008.

AML Program Overview

An MSB's AML program must be written and must address the four "pillars" of a sound AML program:

- Policies, procedures, and internal controls based upon the MSB's risk assessment, which are designed to detect and deter money laundering and terrorist financing;

- Designate a BSA compliance officer and detail the role that person will play in the day-to-day supervision of the MSB;

- Provide for and document policies and procedures to perform independent testing of the MSB to measure compliance with the BSA; and

- Provide for and document BSA/AML training for appropriate personnel.[24]

One MSB emphasized that every employee is responsible for compliance and that division directors are responsible for fostering a strong compliance culture. The MSB's AML program requires officers and/or employees to:

- Comply with BSA and implementing regulations;

- Establish and maintain written standards and procedures;

- Maintain required records;

- Establish, implement, and maintain a customer due diligence and agent due diligence program;

- Monitor transactions, activity, and relationships for suspicious activity;

- Report known or suspected criminal activity; and

- Cooperate with law enforcement, examiners, and regulators within the parameters of applicable law.

---

24. See 31 C.F.R. § 103.125 for anti-money laundering program requirements for MSBs.

Another MSB also stressed that compliance is everybody's responsibility. It views the following as the four "cornerstones" of the compliance program:

- Agent on-boarding;[25]

- A dedicated compliance team;

- Agent supervision and transaction monitoring; and

- Training.

One MSB emphasized its global approach to AML compliance and detection. The MSB deters and detects money laundering and fraud through its internal policies, which include controls that are used to keep its system free from "high risk users" and transactions. Proprietary in-house programs and highly trained staff review accounts and transactions and internal as well as external resources are utilized to recover losses from fraudulent activity.

One MSB has implemented a policy, in addition to a manual exception policy, that prohibits individual transactions from exceeding $10,000. Once the total volume of transactions reaches $2,000, it requires either a Social Security number or the account holder must link the account to another financial institution, such as a bank or credit card.

---

25. Agent on-boarding is generally described as the initial process in which an MSB principal educates and trains the new agent on expectations as to their roles and responsibilities as an agent for the MSB principal

Risk Assessment

An MSB's AML program must be commensurate with the risks posed by the location and size of the particular MSB, and by the nature and volume of the financial services it offers. Each MSB should identify and assess the money laundering risks that may be associated with its unique combination of products, services, customers, geographic locations, etc. Although MSBs are not required by regulation to create a written risk assessment, management is encouraged to document its risk assessment in writing in order to provide a clear basis for the MSB's policies and procedures.[26]

An MSB's BSA/AML risk categories will vary depending on the MSB, but may include product risk, customer risk, geographic risk, and operational risk. As part of the risk assessment, most MSBs will develop a discrete valuation of risk categories (e.g. high, medium, and low) with different business processes or risk mitigation requirements tailored to address the risks in each category.

One MSB noted its enterprise-wide approach to risk assessment of products and services. Customers are risk rated into the following categories: prohibited, high, medium, and low risk. Enhanced Due Diligence (EDD) is performed for high risk customers. This due diligence process includes a site visit, evaluation of beneficiaries, and analysis of customer financials. The MSB also evaluates risks by product and business segments (high, medium, low). This enables it to establish mitigating controls and focus monitoring efforts. For example, this MSB identified banknote services and prepaid card products as higher risk based on individual assessment.

Yet another MSB's risk assessment involves a two-step process – assessing inherent risk, as well as residual risk (after applying risk mitigants) posed by the MSB's customers, agents, correspondents, products, and geographies. Assessing inherent risk involves looking at three areas of risk – regulatory, products/services, and transactional – and applying a four-category weighted risk-ranking system (adverse impact of non-compliance, complexity, visibility, and industry problem). Assessing residual risk involves asking a series of questions for each area, identifying the controls in place to mitigate the risk. The MSB views its overall risk profile as a "low risk business in a high risk industry."

---

26. See http://www.fincen.gov/news_room/rp/files/MSB_Exam_Manual.pdf, p. 19.

In addition, this MSB applies country risk ratings – developing and applying numerical risk scores to all countries in the world, not just the countries in which it operates. Country risk ratings are driven by numerical scores applied to factors such as the country's AML/Counter Terrorist Financing (CFT) legal framework, as well as identification by the Office of Foreign Assets Control (OFAC)[27] or in U.S. government reports such as the U.S. Department of State's International Narcotics Control Strategy Report (INCSR).[28] The MSB also risk rates its sending agents and correspondent/ payout agent locations, considering factors specific to the agent (such as time in business, type of institution, ownership by a politically exposed person, etc.) as well as country factors based on location of registration and operation.

The objective of another MSB's AML program is to identify and assess the AML risks inherent to its business and to develop strategies to mitigate those risks. This MSB revises its risk assessment every 12 to 18 months and strives to mitigate its AML risk in three ways: (1) by knowing with whom it is doing business– agents and consumers, (2) by preventing undesirable activity from entering its system, and (3) by understanding its transaction activity and providing meaningful information to law enforcement. This MSB rates country risk on a 1-4 scale.

The MSB conducts initial due diligence on its agents through an enrollment application process. The amount of background information obtained varies based on structure, but may include convictions, bankruptcies, liens, judgments, license revocations, enforcement actions, terminated relationships with other MSBs, bank history, gambling activities, and a criminal background check.

Customer information is also obtained at the time of the transaction. Money transfer send forms record the destination country, information about the receiver,[29] information about the sender,[30] and the sender's signature. Money transfer receive forms record the amount, information about the receiver,[31] information about the sender,[32] and the receiver's signature.

---

27. See http://www.treas.gov/offices/enforcement/ofac/

28. See http://www.state.gov/p/inl/rls/nrcrpt/2010/vol2/index.htm

29. Amount, name, city and state.

30. Name, address, telephone number, and e-mail address.

31. Name, telephone number, sending location, and address.

32. Name and telephone number.

Another MSB indicated that it conducted a risk assessment with the goal of better understanding the inherent and residual AML risks the customer's business presents to the MSB and outlining how the corporate AML compliance program, resources, and audit activity align with the customer's business risk profile. The risk assessment categories were broken down to: (1) products, services, and delivery methods; (2) agent types; (3) geographies; and (4) entity-wide controls.

To assess transaction risk, one MSB noted that it risk rates both individual transactions and aggregate transactions over different time periods. Additionally, each transaction has certain required fields, with an automated stop mechanism (that can be adjusted by compliance personnel) to prevent a transaction from occurring should a fixed data field not be completed.

Another MSB noted that in order to prevent undesirable activity from taking place through its network, real-time controls are in place to ensure data integrity (i.e., validate consumer data to enhance monitoring and reporting), global/geo-specific controls (e.g., avoid exceeding regulatory requirements in certain jurisdictions), and enhanced customer due diligence to control risk.

At the same MSB, system controls are in place to trigger a request for additional information when transactions exceed certain dollar thresholds. Customers attempting to conduct large transactions or transactions that aggregate to more than $30,000 in a twelve-month period are subjected to enhanced due diligence procedures. This includes connecting the customer over the phone with specialized compliance personnel in the MSB's call center to determine the sender/receiver relationship and source of funds. Potential OFAC matches are also researched by specialized compliance personnel who have the authority to approve or deny transactions.

Independent Review

An MSB's AML program must provide for an independent review of the program in order to assess its effectiveness. Because the independent review need not be a formal audit by a certified public accountant or third-party consultant, an MSB does not necessarily need to hire an outside auditor or consultant. The primary purpose of the independent review is to determine the adequacy of the MSB's AML program, including whether the business is operating in compliance with the requirements of the BSA and the MSB's own policies and procedures.[33]

The internal auditing component of one MSB noted that the MSB's head office places greater importance on reputation and legal risk than credit risk, so AML is a very high priority, especially given the geography of institutions with which the MSB works.

One MSB noted that its internal audit group conducts an annual independent review of the AML program, which consists of transaction testing and assessing employee knowledge.

Another MSB also noted that its independent testing program is completed through internal corporate audits. The MSB's stored value card program is subject to internal corporate audits, including the AML program, and the AML program itself is reviewed by internal auditors.

One MSB indicated that it alternates between its own internal audit and external audit bi-annually. The MSB prepares for independent reviews by conducting compliance exercises that help to identify any possible problems or issues.

Another MSB indicated the annual independent review of its compliance program is conducted by an outside auditing firm.

One MSB discussed how its internal audit program is risk based, looking at entities that have a lot of back-end review findings and entities that have a low volume of forms that are used to report suspicious activity to the compliance group. The audit group visits these entities to find out why the findings are occurring, provides education to the personnel during the visit, and then monitors the situation for 6 months. The efforts for internal auditing are focused on enhancing suspicious activity reporting.

---

33. See http://www.fincen.gov/news_room/rp/files/MSB_Exam_Manual.pdf, p. 52-53

Retail Oversight

One MSB noted that its retail store locations are reviewed approximately every 24 months. The review is more extensive than just AML, as it also includes operations and security. Store employees are quizzed on AML requirements as part of the audit. The audit also includes a review of training records and transaction testing for AML requirements. Depending on the rating of the audit (satisfactory, unsatisfactory, or unacceptable) a follow-up audit is done. For an "unacceptable" rating, the follow-up review is done within 3 months. If the review is rated "unsatisfactory," another review is done in 6 months. "Satisfactory" reviews are repeated again in 24 months.

Remote transaction audits, which test discount fees, commission rates, exchange rates, and reversals, are also performed. Additionally, retail managers must complete new employee checklists, monthly checklists, and a quarterly AML checklist. These checklists are sent to the appropriate compliance personnel for review.

Agent Oversight

All MSBs stressed the importance of oversight of agents not only as critical to their BSA compliance responsibilities, but also as central to their business models. The MSBs noted that agent quality is critical to serving MSB customers and to building and maintaining a reputation for trust and reliability.

While the foregoing premise applied universally, many MSBs noted different legal requirements for their agent relationships in different countries. For example, some countries may limit the ability to establish exclusive agent relationships, or might require different licensing responsibilities, such as money transmission to be conducted through banks. Additionally, in some countries, the amount of publicly available information, coupled with privacy restrictions, may impact the ability to conduct due diligence upon agents.

Similar to the way many financial institutions approach certain ongoing customer relationships, most MSBs view the initial evaluation phase of new agents as the most critical in determining whether the relationship will work out and establishing baseline expectations for ongoing monitoring.

In establishing agent relationships, one MSB noted that it looks for partners that offer complementary products. There are three tiers of oversight for agents (including depository and non-depository financial institution agents). The highest tier of oversight is an on-site visit to the headquarters office and includes a complete review of the AML compliance and training program, as well as a records review. The review takes 1-2 days and a report of findings and recommendations is developed for the agent.

At the same MSB, the second level of oversight is performed on MSB agent branches. The review includes a visit to the agent branches and interviews with employees to determine employee knowledge and understanding of AML program requirements. A final level, which involves the least amount of oversight, is used for domestic financial institution agents selling the MSB's products. This review includes a simple questionnaire that is sent to the agent to complete and is reviewed by the MSB.

Another MSB applies due diligence to send locations and foreign correspondent/ payout locations, including risk assessment, due diligence, training, agent reviews, and "stress tests." The MSB has several agent reviewers and telephonic trainers. In 2008, over 1,000 agent reviews were performed, as well as 2,000 agent trainings. The MSB also utilizes monthly post-transactional analysis to identify agent locations that may be selected for reviews. Agent reviews are announced beforehand for various reasons, including, for example, to ensure that the owner is present.

The review includes an evaluation review of transaction activity, the agent's compliance program, BSA compliance, transaction records, and a training session. An overall rating is developed for the agent. Unsatisfactory compliance may be grounds for agent termination, although the MSB stated that this was infrequent, projecting less than one location closed per month for AML-related reasons. Closures are either credit-related or due to a change in owner (in which case the agent location is re-screened). Common deficiencies noted in agent reviews include independent testing, or not having an AML program tailored to the agent's business. The MSB also utilizes monthly post-transactional analysis to identify agent locations that may be selected for reviews.

Another MSB also noted that its agent oversight program is designed to fully review and evaluate agent compliance with the BSA, State laws, and MSB policies and practices at least once every 12 to 18 months. The agent oversight program is risk-based and driven by transaction analysis and evaluation of additional risk indicators such as previous review history, geography, transaction volume, transaction risk scores, and mystery shopping.

The MSB's agent review process begins with a pre-review transaction analysis followed by a review of the four AML program pillars, a compliance officer interview, training, and program development assistance. Most of the review process is performed off-site through telephone conversations and an exchange of written documentation. On-site reviews generally take a couple of hours to complete and the MSB makes risk-based decisions as to whether onsite work is necessary.

In high-risk geographic areas, the MSB hires former U.S. law enforcement or U.S. intelligence community personnel to conduct due diligence reviews. Most reviews resulting in poor review ratings could result in probation or suspension. The MSB considers an agent's profitability, compliance history, and risk rating in deciding what action to take.

Another MSB also noted its risk-based approach to conducting AML compliance reviews of its agents. Prior to conducting an on-site review, agents are required to take online training so that their compliance knowledge can be gauged. In 2008, over 5,000 agents were reviewed and re-trained in areas of deficiency. Agents may be suspended or terminated for inadequate AML compliance.

One MSB indicated that agent reviews can be either scheduled or unscheduled and are conducted either onsite or over the phone. The highest risk agents receive an onsite visit, lower risk agents receive a phone call, and the lowest risk agents are directed to online training and testing. International agent reviews are not done to the extent as domestic reviews, but the MSB will focus more resources internationally in 2010. The MSB tries to visit 12 percent of domestic agents per year. Agents with AML compliance issues will receive a deficiency letter and additional training. Depending on the severity of the issue and the risk posed by the activity, the AML Compliance Management team has the authority to immediately restrict or terminate an agent.

This same MSB has an enhanced agent review process that is primarily focused on independent agents since most national agents have their own compliance departments. The enhanced process includes transaction analysis, agent risk-ranking, mandatory online training, sweeps of high risk locations, an enhanced compliance kit, and mystery shopping.

Mystery Shopper Visits

As with any aspect of compliance, many of the MSBs articulated that while they focus on establishing BSA/AML policies and training, the key challenge is in the implementation of BSA/AML compliance procedures, including through the agent level. In addition to agent reviews, which are pre-announced, several MSBs noted the use of mystery shopping visits - unannounced "stress tests" designed to gauge the agent's compliance. One MSB indicated that it contracts with firms to visit locations and conduct transactions designed to test the agent's compliance. Locations are selected on the basis of risk, though the MSB does not select the actual locations.

Another MSB also described its use of a mystery shopper program, with its regional compliance officers visiting several agent locations per month through unannounced visits. While the MSB views this program as an emerging industry standard, it also noted that this may not be the most efficient use of the MSB's resources because the reviews are random rather than risk-based and generate findings that may be obtained through transaction analysis. The MSB planned to visit approximately 1,000 agent locations in its 2009 mystery shopping program.

Another MSB noted that its mystery shopping program not only identifies compliance deficiencies but works as a deterrent as agents learn that they might be subject to such visits. The program is expensive so it is not deployed at random.

Customer Identification

A number of MSBs have developed a type of affinity card for their customers that are repeat users. One incentive for customers to use affinity cards might include reduced fees. The information gathered from such customers enables the MSB to pre-populate certain transaction fields, thus increasing speed and accuracy to input transactions.

One MSB described its in-house developed IT system, which automatically prompts agents to enter required data at the point of sale for transactions that have identification requirements (i.e., certain fields become mandatory based on the size of the transaction). These pre-populated drop-down menus build consistency, albeit at the potential risk of one entering a standardized choice instead of a true representation, such as with an open text field. The MSB also utilizes an escalating identification and verification process depending on the size of transactions:

- Collects name, address, and phone number for transactions below $1,000;

- Obtains identification information at $1,000 (the MSB identified this threshold as an industry best practice, and also noted the Financial Action Task Force (FATF) international standards at this level)[34];

- Obtains copy of ID, plus date of birth (DOB), occupation, and Taxpayer Identification Number (TIN) at $3,000; and

- Requests documentary proof of source of funds at $8,000.

The MSB maintains a centralized database for name or address match and watch list screening. The MSB's software has some image capture capabilities enabling AML teams to review identification or other documents.

As mentioned earlier in this report, another MSB noted that once the total lifetime volume of a transaction reaches $2,000, it will require the transactor either to provide a Social Security number or link the account to another financial institution (such as a bank or credit card).

One MSB indicated that all receive transactions require photo identification unless a test question is used to authenticate the receiver for transactions up to $900. Photo identification is recorded in the MSB's system for all send/receive transactions of $900 or greater.

---

34. FATF is an inter-governmental body whose purpose is the development and promotion of national and international policies to combat money laundering and terrorist financing.

Transaction and Activity Monitoring

All MSBs recognized the importance of transaction monitoring, including to identify possible structuring through multiple transactions or agents, as well as to detect suspicious activity.

Automated Alerts

One MSB, in discussing its analytical tool to monitor back-end activity, highlighted that one of the primary benefits of the system was that it reduces reputation risk from compliance related incidents.

Another MSB provided a demonstration of a vendor-developed program used for its retail transaction monitoring. The program is a rules-based system that generates alerts every day, capturing information through the retail system. In 2008, there were over 12,000 alerts generated for business activities within the United States. The MSB has two analysts dedicated to reviewing these alerts, which are given priority rankings from 1 to 10, depending on which rule(s) and how many rules were triggered. The MSB estimates that 20 percent of alerts are false-positives. Analysts must clear an alert or create a case within 5 days. The MSB estimates that 80 percent of the alerts are cleared, 20 percent become cases, and 5 percent result in a SAR filing with FinCEN.

Another MSB noted that it receives both daily and monthly transaction monitoring fraud reports. The MSB takes a proactive approach to its reports and is continually adding new reports and rules and refining the reports. While fraud detection is a part of the MSB's AML program, fraud recovery activities are conducted elsewhere.

To better manage and monitor for risk, another MSB developed proprietary detection and prevention systems that over 1,600 agents monitor and review. Over 200 people within the MSB are dedicated to reviewing activity.

This MSB engages in transaction and account monitoring throughout the life cycle of an account. The MSB has developed forensic and post transaction models to monitor for money laundering and fraud. During the account sign-up process, the MSB scans sanction lists and performs EDD on high risk merchants.

Another MSB's in-house transaction monitoring system detects several patterns, in addition to large and aggregate transaction volume by sender. The system can calculate alerts based on a variety of time frames, ranging from a single day to 360 days.

In addition to transaction monitoring and system alerts, the MSB's agents can flag any transaction as unusual – this will trigger an alert in the company's compliance department, which will investigate the transaction and may contact the agent. Should the company decline to complete a transaction (perhaps due to the customer refusing to provide requested documentation); the company will refund the attempted amount via cash or company-branded check.

Another MSB has developed a decision matrix to assist in researching and reporting potentially suspicious activity. Daily and multiple day monitoring activities are designed to identify and research avoidance of limits, patterns, structuring, unusual usage, multiple brands, high volume/frequency, customer/agent relationships, and multiple locations. Additionally, the MSB has an internal Financial Intelligence Unit (FIU) that is responsible for agent oversight, supporting law enforcement investigations, and 314(b) information sharing.[35] The FIU performs EDD and investigation of high-risk transaction patterns and agents for complicity with questionable activity.

One MSB described a proprietary system developed in-house to assist in monitoring for suspicious activity. Monitoring staff is broken into two groups, with one group responsible for monitoring customers and the FIU responsible for agents. The system is constantly evolving and has been updated multiple times since it became operational based on lessons learned. The system provides analysts with daily referrals of potentially suspicious activity meriting further research.

Another MSB noted its use of sophisticated computer programs to identify unusual money transfer transactions that require closer review by analysts; however, the company also does extensive manual reviews because it cannot rely entirely on the capability of its systems. The MSB's analysts review thousands of money orders and money transfer transactions daily to detect suspicious activity. Suspicious activity involving money orders is detected through the "multiples process" that identifies unusual activity through the clearing process. The MSB indicates that most suspicious activity involves structuring.

Front-Line Referrals

In addition to automated alerts, many of the MSBs noted the importance of referrals received from internal sources. One MSB estimated that in 2008, 50 percent of the unusual activity identified and reported through its internal non-automated suspicious activity reporting process ended up being reported in SAR filings to FinCEN.

---

35. A more detailed discussion of financial intelligence units follows on pg. 23.

Filing BSA Reports

MSBs are required to file CTRs and SARs, as described in more detail later in this report. FinCEN has developed a BSA E-Filing System that supports the electronic filing of BSA forms (either individually or in batches) through a FinCEN secure network, providing a faster, more convenient, more secure, and more cost-effective method for submitting BSA forms to FinCEN.

One MSB that utilizes FinCEN's BSA E-Filing system noted that it files SARs and CTRs for transactions where it is an agent of another MSB. The MSB's agents file CTRs, where required, for products the agent sells while the MSB files CTRs, where required, for products sold to the agents. The MSB indicated that the CTR process is very manual. The MSB is not able to batch-file CTRs because of the complexity of the business.

Another MSB indicated it files SARs (or the equivalent) to global jurisdictions where and when required. The majority of SARs filed by this MSB involve money laundering and/or account takeover.[36] According to the MSB, account takeover is usually accomplished through spoofing or phishing techniques that involve identity theft, credit card, or bank account fraud. The MSB does not deem spoof activity to be suspicious until unauthorized access to an account is confirmed.[37] The MSB then files a SAR based upon the SAR filing requirements and the 30-day time frame as explained in *The SAR Activity Review*, Issue 10.

36. Account takeover is a common form of identity theft, where the criminal is able to obtain enough personal information on the victim to conduct fraudulent transaction on their account.

37. Spoofing and phishing are scams where Internet fraudsters trick victims into disclosing personal and financial information that can be used to steal the victims' identity.

Investigations/SAR Filing Determinations

One MSB noted that trained investigators monitor transactions 24 hours a day, 7 days a week. After an account has been flagged, an investigator will contact the account holder to verify the legitimacy of the transaction. Depending upon the transaction, the investigator may contact the counter-party in the transaction or contact the financial institution that is the funding source for the transaction. If necessary, the investigator will request documents to prove the identity of the account holder. To assist with the investigatory process, the MSB searches public records databases, social networking sites, and open source web search engines. Once all relevant information has been reviewed, an investigator will make a decision on the account or transaction.

Another MSB noted that after unusual transactions are flagged by either agent alerts or transaction monitoring system alerts, dedicated compliance personnel review the alerts, and after further research, either decide to file a SAR, or decide not to file and document the reason for not filing on an internal form. The MSB utilizes a case management system to track alerts and processing. The MSB's compliance officer reads and reviews every SAR before it is filed. The MSB indicated that it has been focusing on improving SAR narratives over the last few years, and stated that it has received positive feedback from law enforcement. The MSB maintains a database of SARs filed, which is used to adjust agent and transaction centric risk models.

Several years ago, one MSB developed a proprietary system to assist in monitoring for suspicious activity. Monitoring is broken into two groups, with one group responsible for monitoring consumers, and the MSB's Financial Intelligence Unit (FIU) responsible for agents. The system is constantly evolving and has been updated numerous times since its inception based on lessons learned. The system provides analysts with daily referrals of potentially suspicious activity meriting further research.

Until recently, one MSB relied solely on a single-level rules matrix to guide its SAR decision-making process. This decision-making process is largely black and white without much allowance for nuance. The MSB's monitoring system is rules based and elevates transactions to analysts when certain conditions are met, with transactions generally permitted to accumulate over a 30-day period prior to review so that trends and patterns can be identified. Analysts reviewing potentially suspicious activity use a decision matrix to answer specific questions that lead to a conclusion as to whether or not to file a SAR. In situations that do not lead to a clear-cut filing decision,

---

analysts use a research table to consider additional factors such as the jurisdictions involved in the activity. The system saves transactions that result in non-filing decisions to reference for future activity.

In 2008, the same MSB launched a suspicious transaction reporting pilot program in Asia. As a result of the pilot program, the average number of transactions per report tripled, the dollar value per report doubled, and the average number of red flag indicators per report increased from 2.9 to 4.9.

The MSB's new reporting model is guided by a dual-level risk matrix that is supported by research and data validity tables. Analysts still review transactions after 30 days for filing decisions but transactions of interest are kept pending for an additional 60 days. The model employs risk- and pattern-based reporting (i.e., serious violations are reported immediately and suspicious patterns are reported when identified). The MSB tested this model in the United States in early 2009. As a result of the program, the average number of transactions per report increased from 5 to 13, the average dollar value per report increased from $12,900 to $19,300, and the average number of red flag indicators per report increased from 3.76 to 4.

Account closure policies

One MSB indicated that in its corporate business relationships, the relationship may be terminated even after one SAR filing, based on the suspected activity. At the retail level, it is difficult to make these determinations given the face-to-face nature of the business with individual customers, particularly since the MSB does not want to put its employees in the position of ending a client relationship.

Approximately every quarter, another MSB will pull a report on customer accounts that have two or more SARs and will determine whether those accounts warrant closure. It appears that this MSB will generally lean toward ending customer relationships that have generated two or more SARs. It also appears, however, that most customers do not reach the point of generating two SARs because most SARs have to do with violations of the MSB's internal policies, which leads to automatic closure.

Another MSB indicated that even after one SAR is filed on a customer; it will not do any further business with the individual (who is placed on "hold"). There is some inherent risk that an individual on hold could do further transactions below detectable thresholds, but the systems in place at the MSB are designed to detect suspicious activity if such activity recurs.

Training

At one MSB, prior to 2008, employee AML training was risk-based. Employees with direct customer access were given 2 weeks from the date of being hired to complete their training, and those with indirect access were given 30 days. Training, which consisted of a slide presentation, was to be completed prior to direct contact with customers.

In 2008, the MSB switched to an online Web-based training, under which every employee needed to complete an online training course twice each year (by June 30 and December 31), regardless of position within the company. The same core module was offered to all employees. The compliance team created the training content and continues to revise the modules.

In 2009, all employees were required to have 90 minutes of annual training. There is one core module to cover the basics and three additional modules to cover the different business divisions, as well as an additional segment for senior management.

There is also a separate module that the MSB provides for its non-bank financial institution agents and depository financial institution agents. The program is set up as a "train the trainer" module to provide training to the responsible person who will subsequently train other employees. A slide presentation is also provided to the agent to facilitate training of agent employees. For some small agents, the MSB has set up the system so that all employees of the agent can access the online training module and take the training. The MSB reviews the online training logs as part of its agent oversight procedures.

Within another MSB, compliance staff members receive frequent informal training in the AML area. Other key employees, such as management staff and others not directly involved in day-to-day operations, receive more formal training on an annual basis. The MSB's sales force is not trained in AML. These staff members can sell products to a client; however, these sales must first go through the MSB's due diligence process.

At another MSB, an external vendor conducts annual BSA training for all employees. The vendor creates an online educational module that tests employees on money laundering schemes that are specific or unique to the MSB. The vendor monitors the testing process, tracks scores, and notifies employees via email that they must complete the online training. Employees receive a certificate after they have successfully completed the training.

In addition to completing the general annual BSA/AML training, managers at the same MSB are required to complete "special compliance overview" training that outlines their responsibilities and helps them identify training for their specific departments. The compliance department develops training for managers, and human resources conducts the training annually. Product, marketing, and legal consultants receive specific job-based AML training in person, and they also receive the general annual BSA/AML training.

The MSB provides specialized, in-person training for members of the board of directors. Members of the board of directors receive the general annual BSA/AML training and they also receive training about their specific responsibilities. The MSB provides the board of directors with compliance program updates once per quarter.

Another MSB's training program is risk-based, with employees divided into high and low risk. Low-risk employees are generally back office, with no customer contact. The MSB provides job-specific training to high-risk employees, and more general awareness training to low-risk employees. Compliance personnel receive monthly training, which may entail seminars and conference calls. Staff members have participated in FinCEN/IRS phone forums, such as the January 2009 call on the rollout of the MSB BSA/AML Examination Manual.

This MSB has produced an AML compliance manual for its employees and agent locations. In-person training is provided prior to activation, as is adoption of an AML program. The MSB stated that it makes agents that offer additional MSB products aware of the need for them to develop their own, specific AML program. The MSB uses FinCEN's MSB video as a new agent tool, and also includes FinCEN MSB outreach materials as part of the "new agent packet." The MSB also provides agents with periodic training materials, such as newsletters and memos advising/reminding agents of requirements or policy changes. Agent training is supplemented with risk-based compliance reviews of agent and correspondent locations.

One MSB notes that it adds approximately 50 new agents per week. Its new agent compliance training consists of AML program development assistance, telephone training prior to activation, 30-minute follow up training after 30 days, and additional 30- to 60-minute training after 120 days, at which time a review is performed. The MSB has found that explaining compliance obligations to agents in their native language is a success factor, since it creates trust, and, therefore, compliance materials are available in 12 languages. The MSB has also found that agents that engage in follow-up training after 30 days experience 50 percent fewer problems than those that do not. Because of this, the MSB would like to make follow-up training a mandatory part of its program.

Another MSB noted its recent development of new, online, interactive training that is targeted based on assessed risks of money laundering and terrorist financing in specific areas. The new annual BSA/AML training consists of several modules and is scenario based. Feedback is given to trainees based on the responses they select. New staff members initially receive 2-4 hours of BSA compliance training.

Another MSB noted that agent training is performed in many ways, such as face-to-face, over the telephone, online, through seminar presentations, manuals and express guides, state-specific guidance, and e-mail support. The MSB partners with several national accounts to collaborate on training/review of store locations, which are customized to reinforce national account and corporate policies. Approximately 13 percent of all U.S. agent locations use the MSB's online training program. Agents are tested through the online program prior to a review in order to gauge their AML compliance knowledge.

Financial Intelligence Unit (FIU)

One MSB explained that its FIU was founded to manage its high-risk agents. Its reviews extend beyond transaction analysis to include EDD, SAR reviews, and extended agent oversight. The FIU receives inquiries and referrals from a variety of internal and external sources, including law enforcement, subpoenas, 314(b) inquiries, research and reporting, agent compliance support, news sweeps, agent network management, corporate security, and agent exception reports. The MSB is a very active 314(b) participant, exchanging information mostly with banks.

Agent reviews performed by the FIU focus on three areas of risk: (1) violation of AML laws, (2) agent or employee complicity, and (3) company policy violations. The reviews may include EDD on agents and principals, retrieval of court documents, hiring of private investigation firms, drafting of custom SAR narratives, and coordination of law enforcement/regulator outreach efforts.

When problems with agents are identified, the FIU considers whether it involves a bad agent, bad agent employees, or bad customer traffic. The FIU also considers whether the agent is complicit or whether it is an issue of training. Once problems are identified, the FIU focuses on what controls are necessary to change the behavior and how the activity can be monitored to assure that it has ceased. Potential responses to identified deficiencies include an immediate agent visit, expanded scope of review, probation, suspension, and termination. Responses always include follow-up monitoring and comprehensive SARs if necessary. The FIU closes 75 to 80 agent relationships per year and files SARs when the termination is related to compliance.

Another MSB noted that one of the company's top priorities for 2010 is to centralize its AML program and build an FIU which will bring together a standardized global AML program as well as dedicated positions for agent oversight.

Law Enforcement Partnership

One MSB described what it considers to be a very responsive relationship with law enforcement. If requested, the MSB can provide law enforcement representatives with a detailed transaction log that contains information on payments sent, payments received, bank withdrawals, and company-branded debit card use.

Additionally, the same MSB will periodically make proactive case referrals to law enforcement on cases it believes should be prosecuted because of either loss to the company or egregiousness.

One MSB indicated that it responds to thousands of requests from local, State, Federal, and international law enforcement agencies, although it does not provide information to law enforcement without first receiving a subpoena or court order. When asked about potential participation in the 314(a) program,[38] management estimated that, because the MSB processes between 250,000 and 500,000 transactions per day and information would have to be pulled from a couple of systems, an additional full-time employee would have to be devoted to the process. However, the MSB is already performing similar data searches for subpoena requests. Searching for exact name matches would be preferable to performing "wild card" searches, but in either case false positive hit resolution will be an issue due to the volume of transactions and the limited amount of identifying information available on record to eliminate false positives.

Another MSB estimates that 95 percent of SARs filed are "technical" in nature, such as structuring, etc. The MSB will occasionally make direct contact with law enforcement, generally placing a first call to the local SAR Review team to get pointed in the right direction.

Two MSBs estimated that they get few requests for supporting documentation from law enforcement – one characterizing the number of requests as a "handful" each year; while another MSB estimates it responds to approximately one subpoena per month from law enforcement.

---

38. See 31 U.S.C. § 5311. Section 314 helps law enforcement identify, disrupt, and prevent terrorist acts and money laundering activities by encouraging further cooperation among law enforcement, regulators, and financial institutions to share information regarding those suspected of being involved in terrorism or money laundering.

Additional Observations

MSB BSA/AML Examination Manual and Examination Issues

As mentioned early in this report, FinCEN released the _Bank Secrecy Act/Anti-Money Laundering Examination Manual_ for Money Services Businesses in December 2008 in order to provide guidance to MSB examiners for compliance with the requirements of the BSA, as well as to provide the MSB industry with information about BSA compliance requirements and examination practices.[39] The manual includes input from a wide variety of sources, including the IRS, the State agencies responsible for MSB regulation, the Money Transmitter Regulators Association (MTRA), the Conference of State Bank Supervisors (CSBS), and FinCEN.

Primary goals of the manual are to enhance BSA examiners' ability to perform risk-based examinations of MSBs, provide a resource to enhance the consistency of BSA examination procedures, and facilitate the efficient allocation of examination resources between Federal and State BSA examiners to ensure consistency in the application of BSA requirements.

FinCEN's meetings with the MSBs took place very shortly after the MSB manual was released. Overall, MSBs stated that the manual is a positive development, emphasizes a standard of reasonableness, and should help improve consistency, while noting that application is key. They also noted that the examination program in the manual can be too much for small agents if not performed in a sufficiently risk-based fashion.

On the topic of examinations and the effectiveness of the manual, several MSBs noted that IRS examiners tend to examine the branches and agents but not the headquarters. Some MSBs noted that improved coordination and centralization of examinations may alleviate the need for the MSB to have to provide the same AML program information to different IRS examiners as the only information that varies from one branch to another is transaction information.

Another MSB noted that while the IRS has not performed an examination of the MSB at the corporate level, extensive examinations are conducted at the agent level. Despite this, the MSB proactively reaches out to the IRS every 18 months to ensure that it is aware of changes within the MSB.

---

39. See http://www.fincen.gov/news_room/nr/pdf/20081209.pdf

In response to this particular issue, as well as some of the others raised by the MSBs regarding examinations, the IRS indicates that it has increased the number of centralized examinations and intends to continue to do so as resources allow.

One MSB also noted that some IRS examiners have visited an MSB's agents without notifying the officials at the corporate level. Also, there is no formal process for corporate officials to receive the results of agent level examinations--the IRS does not issue a report to the corporate officials, so they do not know the results of the agent examination. One MSB commented that the examination cycle and the examiners assigned to perform branch examinations appear to be random.

The IRS indicates that they have begun discussing how to develop an improved process for sharing examination information between MSB agents and principals as appropriate. The IRS also noted that they continue to refine their examination selection process through a risk based process that considers many different factors, including risk-based referrals from FinCEN.

Some MSBs expressed concerns about examinations at the State level, particularly the high number of independent examinations that take place by the States. Many of the MSBs expressed an interest in better coordination of State examinations among multiple states. Further, having multiple States in for examinations takes away from compliance resources.

One MSB noted what it viewed as improving examination coordination between State regulators in recent years and explained that one State regulator in particular will typically take the lead role to coordinate examination activities. In a typical examination conducted by that State, examiners will visit 10 to 20 agent locations prior to the onsite visit. Four to five examiners will then spend 2 to 3 weeks during the onsite portion of the examination at the corporate level. While the MSB was encouraged by the enhanced coordination of examination efforts, officials suggested that a consolidated examination report would also help facilitate coordination in this area.

One of the MSB's biggest concerns is that various States interpret the BSA regulations differently, but another MSB noted that it has started to see decreases in inconsistencies in the examination process among the States since the release of the MSB examination manual. Another MSB expressed optimism that the MSB Examination Manual will help improve the examination process, but that is yet to be seen. Finally, the MSB reported that in at least two States, examiners had said that they had not yet read the MSB examination manual (within the first year of its release).

314(b) Voluntary Information Sharing

Section 314(b) of the USA PATRIOT Act allows regulated financial institutions, including MSBs, to share information with each other for the purpose of identifying and, where appropriate, *reporting possible money laundering or terrorist activity.*[40]

Several MSBs noted that they participate in voluntary information sharing through the 314(b) process. One MSB, however, noted that there may be some confusion within the MSB community about whether MSBs are eligible to participate in 314(b).

One MSB explained that it receives sharing requests from banks, and would also be interested in sharing information with other MSBs about why agent locations are shut down (for AML-related reasons or other reasons, such as credit). The MSB also noted that some financial institutions do not like the administrative requirements of 314(b), such as the requirement to provide notice of their intention to share information with another financial institution.

Another MSB, with which FinCEN met in early 2009, requested further guidance on the use of 314(b) for fraud.

FinCEN understands that some banks were hesitant to share information under the 314(b) program as it related to *suspected fraud*. Following ongoing discussions regarding this issue during these outreach meetings and within the Bank Secrecy Act Advisory Group,[41] FinCEN issued guidance on June 16, 2009 to clarify the scope of permissible sharing covered by the section 314(b) safe harbor.[42] The guidance clarifies that financial institutions, upon providing notice to FinCEN and using procedures designed to safeguard the information, are permitted to share information with one another.

Sharing of information is permitted to identify and report activities, such as suspected fraud — or other specified unlawful activities (SUAs) — if there is a nexus between the suspected fraud or other SUA and possible money laundering or terrorist financing activity.[43] We expect this guidance to result in further exchange of information among financial institutions for the purpose of fighting fraud.

---

40. See 31 U.S.C. § 5311 note; implementing regulations are at 31 C.F.R. § 103.110.

41. The Bank Secrecy Act Advisory Group consists of representatives from State and Federal regulatory and law enforcement agencies, financial institutions, and trade groups.

42. See http://www.fincen.gov/news_room/nr/pdf/20090616.pdf

43. See http://www.fincen.gov/news_room/nr/pdf/20090616.pdf

Maintaining Banking Services

The MSBs recognized FinCEN's efforts to ensure that legitimate MSBs have reasonable access to banking services.

One MSB estimates that it receives approximately 2,000 inquiries a year from agents requesting documentation for their banks in order to obtain or retain banking services. The MSB expressed that while there appeared to be a change in attitude among banks with regard to providing banking services to MSBs after interagency guidance on the provision of banking services to MSBs was published in 2005,[44] there is still a disconnect between the interagency guidance and what bank examiners are looking for, with certain areas of the country presenting particular problems in this regard.

FinCEN Materials

One MSB commented that it has found FinCEN's publications about how to write an effective SAR narrative useful in its reporting efforts. The MSBs also expressed an appreciation for the resources available through FinCEN's website, including publications and information designed specifically for MSBs, such as the educational materials in multiple languages.

---

44. See http://www.fincen.gov/news_room/nr/pdf/20050426.pdf

Additional guidance requested

Prepaid Access

At the time of the outreach visits in 2009, FinCEN was in the process of seeking comments on its existing stored value regulatory provisions and developing a proposal with respect to stored value.

During our meetings, one MSB noted that one of its challenges lies in the differing ways State regulators view stored value, or prepaid access. The MSB also has an interest in whether there will be any differentiation between prepaid access and payroll cards from a regulatory perspective.

Another MSB also expressed an interest in more guidance on prepaid access because compliance personnel are having trouble explaining to company executives why they believe that this is a risky line of business to enter. From a purely compliance model, these individuals believe that a U.S.-only card might be easier to manage.

One MSB noted that around 2004 it noticed that "smarter" criminals were moving to prepaid access. The MSB is challenged to identify prepaid cards that act like credit cards. The MSB stated that credit card networks do not identify which Bank Identification Numbers (BINs)[45] represent prepaid cards; though the MSB indicated that it does not know whether this is because the networks cannot identify such BINs, or because they do not want to provide this information to a competitor.

Another MSB indicated it would be interested in guidance on the treatment of prepaid access. Currently the MSB is treating prepaid access products as negotiable instruments, and is filing SARs when those products are used in a manner that it deems suspicious.

On June 28, 2010, FinCEN issued a Notice of Proposed Rulemaking (NPRM) that proposed new rules to establish a more comprehensive regulatory framework for non-bank prepaid access.[46] The proposed changes are intended to address regulatory gaps that have resulted from the proliferation of prepaid innovations over the last 10 years and their increasing use as accepted payment methods.

---

45. BINs are the primary account numbers found on cards such as credit cards, debit cards, and prepaid access cards. BINs can be used to identify the card issuing institution.

46. See http://www.fincen.gov/news_room/nr/pdf/20100618.pdf

SAR Sharing

One MSB is looking for guidance on the ability of MSB agents and principals to share SARs between themselves. The MSB's interpretation of its ability to do this has fluctuated over the past, and the omission of MSBs from the scope of FinCEN's then proposed guidance on SAR sharing suggested to the MSB that it should not be sharing SARs between affiliates and agents. Clarity on this issue would be helpful to the MSB.

Virtual Currency Operators

One MSB expressed concern that FinCEN has not yet defined as MSBs those entities that provide or facilitate the use of non-currency electronic media of exchange (what the MSB called "virtual currency operators"). The MSB explained that people who are prohibited from opening accounts (or the account is closed at their MSB) move to virtual currency operators and prepaid access issuers, sellers, and redeemers, because there is little to no regulatory oversight for these types of entities. The MSB would like FinCEN to issue guidance on virtual currency.

Conclusion

The meetings allowed FinCEN to learn about the MSBs' programs and challenges, and there was an open and earnest exchange of information and ideas.

During one of the meetings, the MSB's president and CEO stated that FinCEN's outreach initiative was valuable, and stated that this was the first time he had seen an initiative of this nature (i.e. regulator visits outside of the compliance context).

For 2010, FinCEN is conducting similar outreach to some of the nation's depository institutions with assets of less than $5 billion, and to the insurance industry, to learn more about how financial institutions within this asset class implement their AML programs in practice.

Appendix I

Resources Available to MSBs

FinCEN has a section on our website dedicated to information for MSBs, including quick links to useful tools and information designed specifically for MSBs.[47]   One link, in particular, provides users with access to MSB educational materials in English, Arabic, Vietnamese, Farsi, Spanish, Chinese, Korean, and Russian.[48]   Another link takes users to an MSB Registration Renewal Calculator, which provides a means to determine informally the registration renewal dates of an MSB.[49]

Also available on our website, FinCEN periodically publishes *The SAR Activity Review – Trends, Tips and Issues*[50] as a product of close collaboration between FinCEN's regulatory, law enforcement, and industry partners. It is intended to provide meaningful information about the preparation, use, and value of SARs filed by financial institutions. Each issue of The SAR Activity Review provides examples of law enforcement investigations that were assisted by BSA data.

FinCEN's Regulatory Helpline provides assistance to callers from financial institutions, State and Federal regulators, practitioners, law enforcement, and anyone who seeks information about FinCEN or the BSA.[51] MSBs with regulatory questions, such as questions regarding registration status, are encouraged to contact the Regulatory Helpline. MSBs can also contact the IRS-Enterprise Computing Center's Hotline for information about the status of their registration acknowledgment letters.[52]

In addition, FinCEN has issued guidance tailored to MSBs to assist in their compliance with BSA regulations. In October 2007, FinCEN issued guidance to help MSBs enhance the quality of their SAR filings in order for these reports to be as complete and accurate as possible.[53] This information was updated in October 2009

---

47. See http://www.fincen.gov/financial_institutions/msb/

48. See http://www.fincen.gov/financial_institutions/msb/materials.html

49. See http://www.fincen.gov/financial_institutions/msb/calculator.html

50. See http://www.fincen.gov/news_room/rp/sar_tti.html

51. FinCEN's Regulatory Helpline is 1-800-949-2732. For more information on how to contact FinCEN, please see: http://www.fincen.gov/contactus.html

52. The IRS-Enterprise Computing Center-Detroit Hotline is 1-800-800-2877.

53. See http://www.fincen.gov/statutes_regs/guidance/pdf/SAR_Common_Errors_Web_Posting.pdf

with Issue 16 of *The SAR Activity Review*.[54] The issue also contains suggestions from law enforcement for consideration by financial institutions when preparing SARs.

In December 2008, FinCEN released the *Bank Secrecy Act/Anti-Money Laundering Examination Manual*[55] for Money Services Businesses to provide guidance to officials examining MSBs for compliance with the requirements of the BSA. The manual also provides a summary of BSA compliance requirements and examination practices for the MSB industry. The manual made use of input from a wide variety of sources, including the IRS, State agencies responsible for MSB regulation, the Money Transmitter Regulators Association (MTRA), the Conference of State Bank Supervisors (CSBS), and FinCEN.

The manual aims to enhance BSA examiners' ability to perform risk-based examinations of MSBs, provide a resource to enhance the consistency of BSA examination procedures, and facilitate the efficient allocation of exam resources between Federal and State BSA examiners to ensure consistency in the application of BSA requirements. To help make the manual accessible to a greater number of MSBs, on July 19, 2010, FinCEN also released a Spanish language translation of the manual.[56]

In May 2009, FinCEN issued a proposal to revise the regulations implementing the BSA regarding MSBs in order to, among other things, clarify which entities are covered by the definitions.[57] In crafting the proposal, FinCEN reviewed the MSB regulatory framework with a focus on providing efficient and effective regulation for the industry, as well as improving the ability of regulators, law enforcement, and FinCEN to safeguard the U.S. financial system from the abuses of terrorist financing, money laundering, and other financial crime.

The proposed changes are intended to more clearly define the categories of MSBs, so that determining which entities are obligated to comply will be more straightforward and predictable. The proposal would amend the current MSB regulations in the following ways:

- By making clear that certain foreign-located entities doing MSB business in the United States (through instrumentalities such as the Internet) are subject to the BSA rules; and

---

54. See http://www.fincen.gov/news_room/rp/files/sar_tti_16.pdf

55. See http://www.fincen.gov/news_room/nr/pdf/20081209.pdf

56. See http://www.fincen.gov/news_room/rp/files/MSB_Exam_Manual_Spanish.pdf

57. See http://edocket.access.gpo.gov/2009/pdf/E9-10864.pdf

- By updating the MSB definitions to reflect past guidance and rulings, current business operations, evolving technologies, and merging lines of business.

FinCEN provides funding to the IRS for a group of BSA specialists who offer free educational outreach and products to assist MSBs in complying with the BSA regulations. The IRS BSA outreach team has created a model that focuses on, but is not limited to, recognizing and reporting suspicious activities and implementing an effective AML compliance program. None of these programs, however, should replace the standard training requirements of an MSB's BSA/AML program.

The IRS BSA outreach team has also created a model for banks and other depository institutions to use in providing focused outreach to their MSB customers. In an effort to increase compliance with the BSA, MSB customers are invited to receive training on the registration, reporting, and recordkeeping requirements.

In an effort to leverage resources, the IRS BSA outreach team is also actively pursuing opportunities to conduct joint outreach with State banking departments with the purpose of increasing awareness of the BSA and its requirements within the MSB industry.

Additional information about the MSB reporting and recordkeeping requirements can be obtained by calling the IRS BSA specialist in your geographical area.[58]

---

58. See http://www.irs.gov/businesses/small/article/0,,id=148831,00.html

Appendix II

Acronym List

AML	Anti-Money Laundering
BINs	Bank Identification Numbers
BSA	Bank Secrecy Act
CSBS	Conference of State Banking Supervisors
CFT	Counter Terrorist Financing
CTR	Currency Transaction Report
EDD	Enhanced Due Diligence
FATF	Financial Action Task Force
FinCEN	Financial Crimes Enforcement Network
FIU	Financial Intelligence Unit
INCSR	International Narcotics Control Strategy Report
IRS	Internal Revenue Service
MLCA	Money Laundering Control Act
MSB	Money Services Business
MTRA	Money Transmitter Regulators Association
OFAC	Office of Foreign Assets Control
SAR	Suspicious Activity Report
SAR-MSB	Suspicious Activity Report by Money Services Business
SUA	Specified Unlawful Activity
TIN	Taxpayer Identification Number